NATIONAL MUSEUM OF ANTHROPOLOGY

photography

Adrián García Valadés
Silvia Gómez Tagle
Lourdes Grobet

text
Silvia Gómez Tagle

GV
editores

10a. edition, 1993.

Dealer: Grupo Cultural Especializado, S.A. de C.V.
Av. Popocatépetl 510, México 03330, D.F.
Tel: 688-28-41   688-98-31

COVER

Chalchiuhtlicue – goddess of water– in the square of the **Pyramid of the Moon.**

Contents

CHRONOLOGY OF THE NATIONAL MUSEUM OF ANTHROPOLOGY

1790	The Sun stone (also called the Aztec Calendar) and the statue of Coatlicue are discovered in the main square in Mexico City, then known as the Plaza de Armas.
1865	Maximilian, Emperor of Mexico, signs an agreement under which the National Museum is installed on Moneda Street in Mexico City.
1939	During the presidency of Lázaro Cárdenas, Alfonso Caso promotes the foundation of the National Institute of Anthropology and History (Instituto Nacional de Antropología e Historia).
1940	The National Museum on Moneda Street is dedicated exclusively to the exhibition of anthropological collections under the auspices of INAH. The National School of Anthropology and History, linked to INAH, is founded.
1964	On September 17 President Adolfo López Mateos inaugurates the new building of the National Museum of Anthropology, located at Paseo de la Reforma and Calzada Gandhi. Construction is carried out under the direction of architect Pedro Ramírez Vázquez, with the collaboration of 52 architects and 42 engineers. The building spans 44,000 covered and 35,000 uncovered square meters, together with outside gardens and parking areas, making a total area of 125,000 square meters.

Introduction

The study of the native people of Mexico, their languages, their religions and their customs, dates back to the colonial period. Shortly after the Conquest, the Spaniards began to collect information on those cultures they termed "indigenous", to better understand the peoples under their rule. Thus frequent references are made to an anthropological tradition in Mexico that dates back to the sixteenth century.

After Mexico gained its independence, anthropology played a central role in the development of a national consciousness, that recognized the mixture of two great cultural traditions –the pre-Hispanic and the European–. Since the Revolution of 1910 the concept of national identity has been reappraised and redefined so that the most important components are the pre-Hispanic past and the indigenous cultures of the present Thus, the significance of anthropological research has come to be acknowledged, and the government has become interested in the dissemination of information on archaeological finds.

The National Museum of Anthropology symbolizes the importance accorded to anthropology in our country, through the variety and extraordinary richness of the

The main entrance to the museum and the fountain from the esplanade.

collections on exhibit, as well as through the grandeur of the building that houses them. The general plan of the museum reflects the influential role of anthropology, for it is based on an ideological concept that has its roots in the Mexican Revolution.

Despite the diversity of the archaeological trends to which the archaeologists, social anthropologists, linguists, physical anthropologists and ethnologists participated in the initial phases of the museum and collaborated in the task of conservation since its foundation belonged or belong, it can be said that the museum not only displays collections of great artistic beauty, but also attempts to give an overall view of the cultures of pre-Hispanic Mexico and of the ethnic groups that today preserve the roots of that distant past. For these reasons it is, without doubt, one of the most important museums of its type, and the one that best gathers those pre-Hispanic and contemporary elements that make up the Mexican nation.

The basic purpose of the museum is to exhibit everything connected with anthropology in Mexico. The twelve halls on the lower level are dedicated to archaeological exhibits from pre-Hispanic cultures that flourished in the area now occupied almost entirely by the Republic of Mexico. On the upper level are twelve halls that exhibit ethnographical material from the principal contemporary indigenous groups. A detailed description and floor plans of the museum are found on pages 14 and 15.

At the entrance to the museum on the Paseo de la Reforma, stands a famous –probably unfinished– monolith. It was found in what was apparently the quarry from which the stone was taken near Coatlinchán in the hills bordering eastern Valley of Mexico. This statue pertains to the Teotihuacan culture and probably represents the rain goddess, Chalchiuhtlicue, although it is sometimes called Tlaloc, the rain god.

At the main entrance to the museum, an Orientation Hall (no. 17 on the floor plan) can be found in the vestibule. Here a panoramic vision of Mesoamerica is presented by means of light, sound, dioramas, architectural models and photographic media of the cultures that developed there.

To the right of the vestibule is the Torres Bodet Auditorium, (no. 16) the Temporary Exhibitions Hall, (no. 15) and the Ticket Office, where guide service is available in several languages and can be hired to take visitors around the museum.

To the left are the general offices, the checkroom, public telephones, and the museum shop where books and native crafts are sold. (no. 14)

On the upper floor to the left of the entrance hall is the National Library of Anthropology, which houses a very valuable collection of books and ancient manuscripts, including various codices. (no. 11)

In the basement is another small auditorium and the Educational Services office which offers various courses for children. Also in the basement are the cafeteria and the restaurant.

On the upper and basement levels to the right of the entrance are the departments of linguistics, ethnohistory, archaeology, ethnography and physical anthropology, laboratories for restoration, photography, ceramics, as well as storage rooms.

On leaving the main hall at street level, one enters a courtyard of monumental proportions, which brings to mind the use of vast open spaces in the urban works of pre-Hispanic architects. All of the halls on the ground level, open directly off this great courtyard in such a way that the visitor can begin the tour in any one of them.

A huge structure covers part of the courtyard like an inverted umbrella to protect it from the elements. An aluminum roof measuring 52 by 84 meters is suspended from a central column 11 meters in height. This column is decorated with bronze bas-reliefs, the work of the muralist Chávez Morado. Around it falls a curtain of water.

At the other end of the courtyard is a pond that contains marsh vegetation similar to that which existed in the lake where the Aztecs founded Tenochtitlan. On a platform at the end a bronze conch shell reproduces the sound of pre-Hispanic conches.

Central courtyard of the museum. Above: a pool with marsh vegetation which recalls the place of origin of the Mexican Culture.

Below: The huge fountain known as the umbrella. The central column is decorated with bas-reliefs representing, on one side, elements of pre-Columbian culture and on the other, aspects of Western culture.

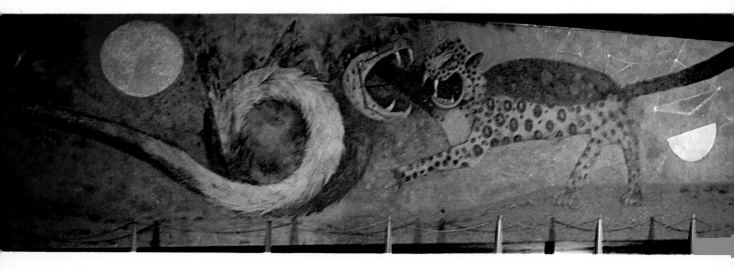

Main entrance hall of the museum. Mural by Rufino Tamayo, the principal subject of which is based on the mythology of the pre-Columbian cultures. It depicts the struggle between positive powers, represented by Quetzalcoatl (the feathered serpent), and the negative symbolized by Tezcatlipoca. The two figures have day and night as a background.

SERVICES

MUSEUM VISITING HOURS
    Tuesday to Saturday: 9:00 A.M. - 7:00 P.M.
    Sunday: 10:00 A.M. - 6:00 P.M.
    Monday: closed

ORIENTATION HALL
    First showing at 11 o'clock; repeated every 25 minutes.

TEMPORARY EXHIBITION HALL
    Mexican and foreign archaeological pieces exhibited for short periods.

GUIDE SERVICE
    Spanish, English and French tours available for groups of .at least 5 people. Free in Spanish; low fee is charged or English .and French guides.

EDUCATIONAL SERVICES
    Trained teachers lead groups of school children visiting the museum. Prior registration in the offices of INAH (Córdoba 45, Col. Roma) is required.

LIBRARY
    Open to the general public; identification is required.
    Schedule: Monday to Friday: 9:00 A.M. - 8:45 P.M.
    Saturday: 9:00 A.M. - 1:00 P.M.
    Sunday: 8:30 A.M. -1:00 P.M.

BOOKSTORE
    Open to the public during museum hours. Specialized books and Mexican handicrafts available.

CHECKROOM
    Bags, packages, photography equipment, coats, etc. may be checked free with entrance ticket.

RESTAURANT AND CAFETERIA
    Open to the public during museum hours.

WHEELCHAIR SERVICE
    Available to disabled and elderly people.

PARKING
    Free with entrance ticket.

Introduction to Anthropology

The contact of the Western world with the peoples of other continents has, at different moments in time but particularly since the expansion of capitalism in the eighteenth and nineteenth centuries, awakened an interest in the study of customs, languages, ways of thinking, and so on. Through an awareness of this apparent diversity of social and cultural expression, a series of reflections and conclusions concerning the nature of humankind emerge.

Anthropology as a discipline attempts to bring together the expertise of different specialists to propose explanations of the relationship between people, nature and culture. The development of this relationship has been a lengthy process, extending over several hundred thousand years, from the evolution of the first

Mural by Jorge González Camarena, inspired by the anthropological theme "Culture is the Heritage of All Races." In the lower part are cultural elements of all the continents; in the upper part are women representing different physical types

primates, forerunners of the human race, to humanity's diversification through numerous and complex processes of interaction with its surroundings during the last fifty thousand years.

Studies have demonstrated that all cultures, even those that possess the most elementary technology, satisfy the basic needs of the species, both physiologically and psychologically. Therefore, it is difficult to conclude that some cultures are "superior" to others. Physical anthropology has also helped to disprove the theory that alleges the superiority of the white race by uncovering the fundamental unity of physiological characteristics and evolutionary processes. The mural entitled "Culture is the Heritage of All Races", by Jorge González Camarena, expresses this concept.

In the section of the museum dedicated to physical anthropology there are a number of reproductions of bone fragments, graphs and sketches that illustrate the biological evolution of primates to the present species. This group also includes the hominids who gave rise to the human race and to other species such as apes and monkeys.

Linguistics is the branch of anthropology dedicated to the study of human forms of communication as a symbolic means of transmitting knowledge and abstract ideas. This attribute, the ability to transmit instructions, is possessed solely by the human race to the exclusion of other hominids.

Archaeology deals with the material remains of ancient cultures and, by means of systematic study, attempts to reconstruct the lifestyle and social structure of a people. In this hall one can find photographs of archaeological excavations, together with the tools and techniques employed by archaologists.

In another section a general idea of the evolution of culture is presented, from the prehistoric hunters and gatherers to the civilizations of Mesopotamia, Egypt, China, India, Mesoamerica and Peru. It is interesting to note the strong similarities existing in the remotest periods of prehistory between all hunter-gatherers, in their stone tools, the earliest ceramic ware, and the first instruments for plant cultivation, as well as the evergrowing differences between the races as their cultures became more complex and specialized.

The final portion of the hall is dedicated to ethnology. Generally speaking, this science has dedicated itself to the study of so-called primitive cultures, that is to say, those that have not achieved a high level of technological development. However, our planet's ever-accelerating rate of integration in a finite space, combined with a lessening of the gap between rich and poor, governors and governed, tends to break down the barriers between ethnological and sociological studies. Furthermore, by examining the cultures of other peoples and other ages, anthropology can also make a significant contribution to an understanding of contemporary society, especially in a country such as Mexico, a nation made up of such a diverse mixture of peoples.

Mesoamerica Hall, in which are exhibited objects representative of the cultures that flourished in this region. At the end is a mural by Raúl Anguiano, which represents the religious concepts of the Mayas. (photograph on page 11).

Mesoamerica Hall

This hall combines the characteristic elements of the cultures that flourished in pre-Hispanic Mexico. In the chronological table on the following page we can find the cultures that occupy the archaeological halls of the museum, together with their corresponding dates in Mesoamerica an outstanding process of continuous cultural development took place and important urban centers appeared. It has been customary to divide this cultural development into three great eras or "horizons": the Preclassic (1700 - 200 B.C.); the Classic (200 B.C. - A.D. 900); and the Postclassic (A.D. 900 until the arrival of the Spaniards). Each horizon has been subdivided into shorter periods, like the Early Preclassic.

Date	Horizon	Period	Mesoamerica	Prehistoric Origins	Preclassic	Teotih
					CENTRA	
1 520	POSTCLASSICAL	Late				
1 000		Early				
	CLASSICAL	Late				
		Early				
		Protoclassical				
A.D. 0 B.C.	PRECLASSICAL	Upper				
1 000		Middle			TLATILCO ZACATENCO EL ARBOLILLO	TEOTIHUACAN
		Lower				
	ORIGINS					

TABLE
AT THE MUSEUM HALLS

Toltec	Mexica	Oaxaca	Gulf Coast	Mayan	Northern Mexico	Western Mexico

H L A N D S

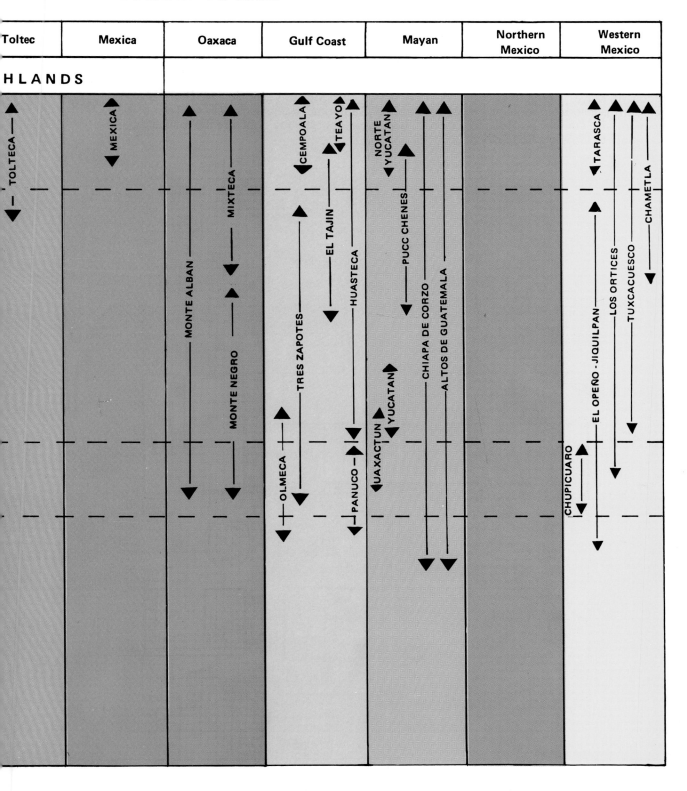

Lower floor of the museum

Lower floor of the museum. 1. Introduction to Anthropology. 2. Mesoamerica. 3. Prehistoric Origins. 4. Preclassic period in Central Mexico. 5. Teotihuacan. 6. Toltec. 7. Mexica. 8. Oaxaca. 9. Gulf of Mexico. 10. Maya. 11. Northern Mexico. 12. Western Mexico. 13. Vestibule. 14. General offices checkroom, public telephones and museum shop. 15. Temporary Exhibitions Hall. 16. Torres Bodet Auditorium. 17. Orientation Hall. 18. Stairs to the lower floor; to the right are the restaurant and coffee shop; to the left is Educational Services.

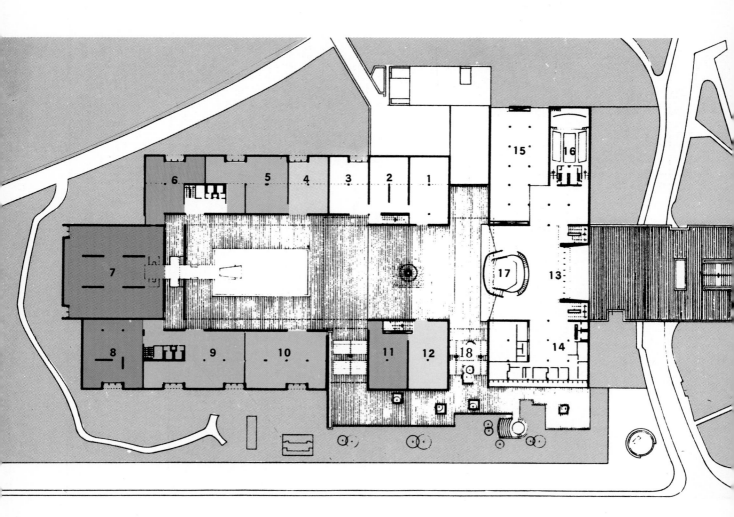

Upper floor of the museum

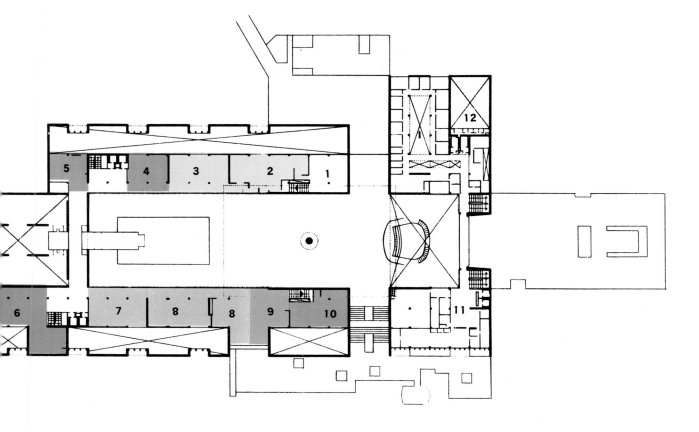

Upper floor of the museum. 1. Introduction to Ethnography. 2. Coras and Huichols. 3. Purépecha. 4. The Otomiano Groups. 5. Sierra de Puebla. 6. Oaxaca. 7. Gulf Coast. 8. The Mayan groups. 9. Northwest Mexico. 10. Nahua groups. 11. Library. 12. Research offices.

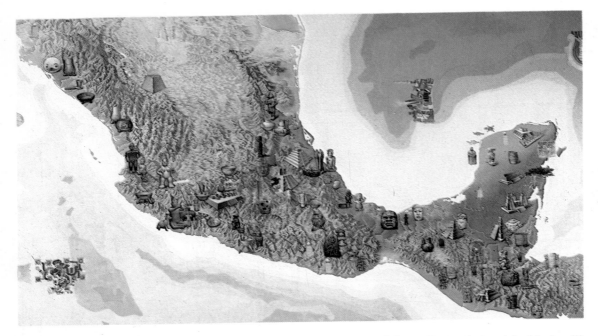

Mural of a map of Mesoamerica representing typical elements of the cultures that existed in its different areas: Central Plateau, Gulf, Oaxaca, Maya, West and North.

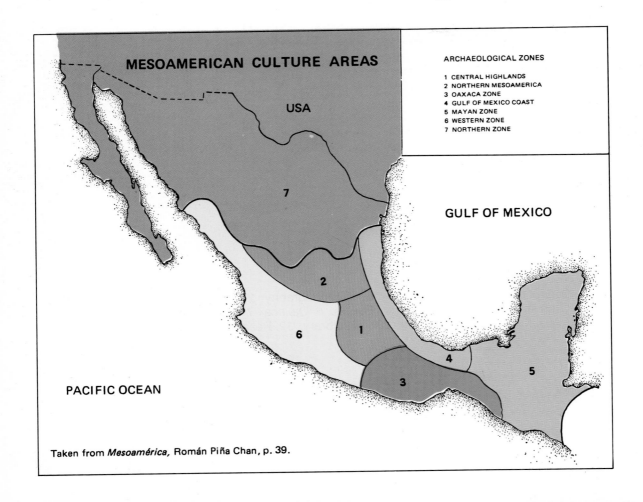

MESOAMERICAN CULTURE AREAS

ARCHAEOLOGICAL ZONES

1 CENTRAL HIGHLANDS
2 NORTHERN MESOAMERICA
3 OAXACA ZONE
4 GULF OF MEXICO COAST
5 MAYAN ZONE
6 WESTERN ZONE
7 NORTHERN ZONE

USA

GULF OF MEXICO

PACIFIC OCEAN

Taken from *Mesoamérica,* Román Piña Chan, p. 39.

A close-up of the mural by José Chávez Morado. It symbolizes the development of Mesoamerican culture in the Preclassic, Classic and Postclassic periods. A general view of the Mesoamerican Hall with the map of the region in the background.

Mesoamerica has been divided into five areas: the Central Plateau, the Gulf Coast, Western Mexico, the Oaxaca area, and the Maya region. The cultures of the Central Plateau occupy four halls: the Preclassic, Teotihuacan, Tula and Xochicalco, and Mexica (Aztec). There is one hall for each of the other areas, as well as one for the cultures of Northern Mexico, which belong to so called America.

The halls on the ground level (p. 14) are indicated with the same colors that denote the corresponding period on the chronological chart on pages 12 and 13. The ethnographic halls on the upper floor are colored to match the areas of origin on the map on page 16.

Mesoamerica is the name given to the area that includes the greater part of the present-day Republic of Mexico and that is bounded to the north approximately by the Pánuco and Sinaloa rivers, extending to the south to include Guatemala, northwestern Honduras, Western Nicaragua and Costa Rica. This region was characterized in pre-Hispanic times by a continual settlement of sedentary agricultural peoples, important cities builders and creators of a varied and complex culture. Further to the north, other urban cultures existed, such as that of Casas Grandes in Chihuahua or that of the Pueblo Indians in the United States, but these did not achieve the importance of the Mesoamerican cities. The frontiers of Mesoamerica were not always the same; they altered with the climatic changes that interfered with agricultural activities or with human migrations. Generally speaking, it is thought that the hunters and gatherers moved south from North America.

The permanent settlements of Mesoamerica were characterized by agriculture based on the cultivation of corn, beans, squash, chile and other domestic plants and fruit; the construction of important buildings in the city centers for the use of priests and rulers, a high level of production of lapidary goods, ceramics, mural paintings, and codices; and the use of the calendar. These traits constitute more than a collection of material remains of cultures. They testify to an ability to produce goods promoted by ecologically favorable conditions that permitted the maintenance of societies with complex political or-

ganization from the early Preclassic period (3,000 B.D.) until the sixteenth century Spanish Conquest.

These societies would have been divided into social classes, with a marked difference in political power and material wealth between the nobles, priests, military leaders, and the rest of the population. In the larger cities the merchants, warriors, artists and artisans probably formed an intermediate class, with peasants and unskilled workers on the lower rungs of the social ladder

The Mesoamericans were farmers par excellence, although they also engaged in fishing, hunting and the collection of natural foods to supplement their diet. All this is shown to the visitor by means of tableaux and showcases that demonstrate cultivation techniques and the tools utilized in these tasks.

On exhibit are ceramics characteristic of the style of each culture, such as vases from Teotihuacan, Zapotec urns, and bowls from Chupícuaro.

Similar gods were worshiped in each region with similar rites, but the deities were known by different names. Raúl Anguiano's mural shows the basic elements of religious belief among the Mesoamerican peoples. There is also a section for different funerary customs.

The mural by José Chávez Morado represents the most important moments of Mesoamerican cultural development. The intellectual and scientific achievements of these peoples are illustrated by means of drawings of their development of a calendar of 365 days, writing, mathematics, astronomy, architecture, metalworking, sculpture, lapidary work, and so on.

Jewelry and metalwork using shell, bone, wood and semiprecious stones are also displayed.

Last, there are models to illustrate some of the typical structures of the pre-Hispanic peoples, from the most elementary temple foundations to the important and complex buildings forming the center of great cities such as Teotihuacan.

Prehistoric Origins

Up to the present, the most commonly accepted theories maintain that America was populated by means of a series of migrations from Asia. The route was over the Bering Strait during the last glacial period, when ice masses formed a bridge linking the two continents.

These groups of migrants were basically nomadic and lived from hunting, fishing and the collection of wild fruit. They were familiar with the use of fire and possessed rudimentary stone implements.

Stone objects on exhibit show the different periods of technological evolution: Archaeolithic (30000 - 12000 B.C.); Lower Cenolithic (12000 - 7000 B.C.); Upper Cenolithic (7000 - 5000 B.C.); and the Protoneolithic (5000 - 2500 B.C.)

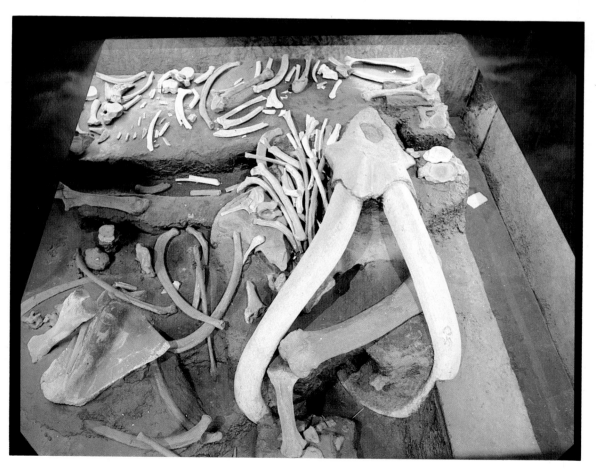

Scale model of the excavation of a mammoth found at Santa Isabel Ixtapan, state of Mexico, in 1954. This show a young animal, hunted and dismembered approximately 12000 years ago.

Above: Mural by Iker Larrauri entitled "Pleistocene fauna in Mexico," with a series of gigantic animals that existed in Mexico thousands of years ago.

Stone implements utilized by hunters in the Protoneolithic or Incipient Agricultural Age (5000 - 2500 B.C.)

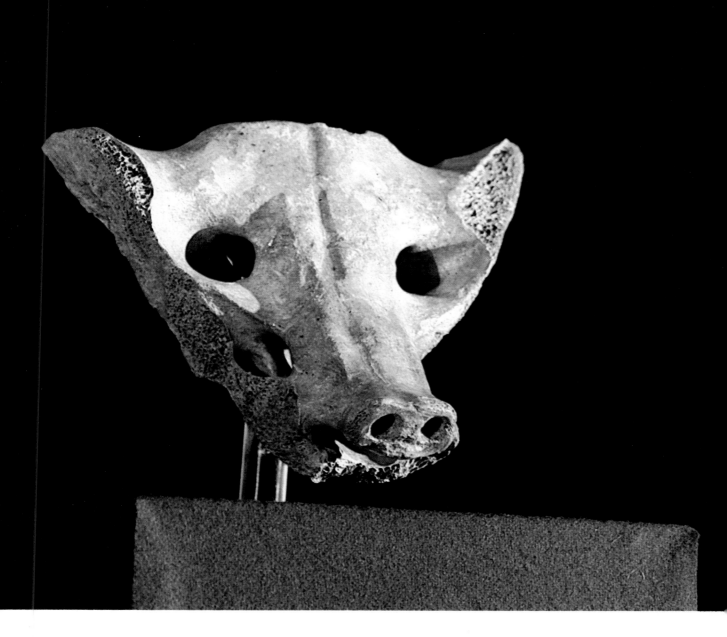

Fossilized sacrum found in Tequixquiac (state of Mexico) and estimated to date from about 12000 B.C. It is a sacrum that prehistoric man formed into an animal head; thus, it is considered to be the earliest known sculpture of the Americas and without doubt, one of the most outstanding pieces in the Prehistoric Origins Hall.

During the Protoneolithic period, humanity went through a transition from a nomadic existence to the beginnings of a sedentary life, dedicated principally to agriculture. The cultivation and domestication of plants such as corn, squash, beans, and chile, among others, commenced at this time.

A large mural painted by Iker Larrauri shows the fauna of the Pleistocene age in Mexico. In front of

the mural is a sunken area containing a reconstruction of the discovery of the fossilized remains of a mammoth, that was hunted and cut up by primitive people in the Valley of Mexico. There is also a diorama of a mammoth hunt in the swamps surrounding Lake Tepexpan by the men who inhabited the valley toward the end of the Archaeolithic age and at the beginning of the Lower Cenolithic age. A nearby case contains human bone remains that

Stone artifact for grinding, called a *molcajete*, belonging to the Protoneolithic age in Mexico (5000 - 2500 B.C.). Besides representing a great advance in stone-carving techniques, the presence of stones to grind grain indicates the existence of an incipient agriculture, hence the name "Protoneolithic."

show the different craneological types of the early inhabitants of Mexico. In other parts of the hall one can see remains of prehistoric animals such as a gigantic jawbone that probably belonged to a mammoth.

There are also stone objects that illustrate the evolution of Mexican culture, from them one can appreciate the change from nomadic gatherer to sedentary, incipient farmer. Some items of ceramic ware which form the earliest examples of the potter's craft in Mexican prehistory, and fossils of the first domesticated plants, including corn, are on display as well.

Preclassic Period in Central Mexico

Clay representation of a dancer found in Tlatilco, state of Mexico, and belonging to the Middle Preclassic period.

That long period of antiquity during which the agricultural cultures underwent continual change until they reached their zenith is known as the Preclassic Horizon. In the Central Plateau, which is the region to which this hall is principally dedicated, the Preclassic period is divided into three eras: the Lower Preclassic (1700 - 1300 B.C.), the Middle Preclassic (1300 - 800 B.C.), and the Upper Preclassic (800 - 200 B.C.)

During the Lower Preclassic, traces of sedentary life began to appear, with the creation of villages probably inhabited seasonally. With the development of more productive agriculture, the construction of permanent villages began in the Valley of Mexico, together with the production of ceramic ware and other handicrafts. The first villages appeared on the shores of lakes, as was the case with Tlatilco, Zacatenco and El Arbolilllo. Archaeologists have shown that during this period funerary practices became more complex, which possibly means evolution of religious beliefs. It is also probable that a process of social differentiation began to develop with the advent of sedentary life, with the upper levels of the social hierarchy occupied by priests and warriors. Unfortunately the material remains that archaeologists have to work with offer little information about social structure. However, when we consider details of "primitive" contemporary communities, it is easy to suppose that blood ties were an important factor in those first agricultural settlements, where the concentration of political power in a social group or class had not yet evolved to allow one to speak of the establishment of a State.

Later, in the Upper Preclassic period, the first pyramidal foundations were laid for temples, and hieroglyphic writing, numbers and the calendar began to be used. These cultural events undoubtedly reflect the existence of reasonably important cities and of differentiation between social groups by specialized activities and by political influence. This is probably when the State came into existence.

The hall is divided into three sections, one for each era of the Preclassic period –in which the ceramic sequence is demonstrated with pieces of great beauty. In the first section, to the right, are items belonging to the Lower Preclassic period, such as earthenware figurines, pots for water storage, jugs, and plates found at El Arbolillo, Zacatenco and Tlatilco, among others.

The ceramic sequence continues with pieces from the Middle Preclassic. There is a marked Olmec influence during this period originating in the Gulf Coast, which possibly enriched the potter's art of the Central Plateau. By means of their realism, the figures of this period provide us with information about the physical type of the settlers, their dress and their ornaments, including cranial deformation, tattooing, hairstyles, body and facial painting, and the like.

We know that they worshiped natural phenomena and fertility. In this section are pregnant female figurines, offerings for a good harvest. Outstanding in the center of the hall is the reconstruction of an interesting burial found at Tlatilco, which shows the funerary practices of the period.

The final portion of the hall contains a display of ceramics dating from the Upper Preclassic. Here one finds more variety in form and decoration than for previous ceramics and some pieces reflect an influence from northern areas such as Chupícuaro and Guanajuato. During this period, for the first time instruments for construction appear. Outstanding among these are hammers, plumb bobs, chisels and perforators, indicating a high level of technological development.

The hall ends with an exhibit of Upper Preclassic objects from places such as Tlapacoya, Zacatenco, Ticoman, Teotihuacan and other areas of Mesoamerica.

Clay figure with feline facial traits. It represents a personage dressed in a jaguar skin and belongs to the Middle Preclassic period. Found at Atlihuayan, Morelos.

Clay mask of a human face. This represents the duality of life and death and expresses the magic-religious beliefs of the Middle Preclassic period. Found at Tlatilco, state of Mexico.

Small clay figurine used as a propitiatory offering for good crops. It represents a man with a ball of dough between his hands, and belongs to the Middle Preclassic period.

The figurines of the Middle Preclassic period show, in part, the physical characteristics of people at that time, as well as their dress, ornaments, and hairstyles. Plaits and locks of hair were common and could have been used either for beautification of to distinguish the user.

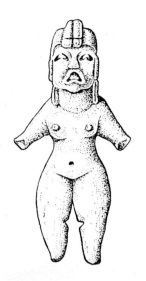

Some kinds of figurines from the Mid Preclassic. From Román Piña Chan, *Mesoamérica,* 1960, p. 63.

Clay acrobat or contortionist, with Olmec influence demonstrated in the facial features. It belongs to the Middle Preclassic period and measures 22 cm in height. It was found at Tlatilco, in the state of Mexico.

Teotihuacan Hall

One of the most important cities of the Classic period (200 B.C - A.D. 900) in Mesoamerica was Teotihuacan, which means "the Place where Men Became Gods". This valley had been inhabited since Preclassic times, and probably began to develop into an urban center, but it was not until around 100 B.C. that one could begin to speak definitely of the existence of a very well planned city with an administrative and ceremonial center built along a main avenue, afterwards called the Avenue of the Dead.

This great city extended its domination and cultural influence to many regions of Mesoamerica, and was also a commercial center where agricultural products and handicrafts were gathered from places as distant as the Mayan regions of Guatemala.

The mass production of ceramics, the carving of stone, and in particular the manufacture of cutting and piercing instruments made of obsidian occupied much of the population of Teotihuacan, as has been confirmed by archaeological studies carried out in the residential areas of the site. It should be remembered, however, that other activities, such as basket making and the weaving of cotton, almost certainly existed, but have not left such obvious archaeological traces.

The tour of the hall begins with an interesting marker used in the ball game. It consists of sections superimposed on each other, and is known as the "Stela of La Ventilla", as it was found in La Ventilla.

Next, we have an architect's model of the valley and the city of Teotihuacan. The first great pyramid to be built was the Pyramid of the Sun, followed by the Pyramid of the Moon, which is constructed at a higher elevation in such a way that it appears to be the same height even though it is actually smaller. The city was built with a north-south axis, deviating 15° 30' east, from the astronomical north, and another axis running east-west. The first, which is two kilometers in length, was the most important and is known as the Avenue of the Dead. It begins in the extreme south near the Citadel and ends at the Plaza of the Moon in the extreme north. The entire length of this avenue is flanked by the palaces of the priests and rulers, by administrative buildings, and by temples.

During its period of greatest splendor, around the seventh century of our era, Teotihuacan had approximately 80,000 inhabitants and covered a surface area of 20 square kilometers. Its planning was outstanding, with streets laid out along the north-south and east-west axes, and with houses built on cement foundations even outside the area of the religious administrative center, etc. All of the foregoing indicates the existence of a very complex social, economic and governmental system.

Teotihuacan pottery in a wide variety of shapes and styles, typical of each period, is exhibited in the glass showcases. A section is also dedicated to implements utilized in building, basket weaving and the like, which demonstrate the high level of technological knowledge.

A display in the center shows some of the utensils employed for domestic use, such as the huge pots for grain storage, amphoras for water, cooking vessels and braziers.

On the right-hand side of the main hall is an outstanding reproduction of the Temple of Quetzalcoatl or the Plumed Serpent, painted in the original colors with which the stucco was decorated. The original is located in the Citadel of Teotihuacan. The side walls of the hall show reproductions of some of the more famous murals, such as the "Tlalocan", showing scenes of daily life among the Teotihuacan inhabitants.

There are also some large sculptures that represent different aspects of the religion of Teotihuacan, and huge photographs of architectural elements typical of the city.

The last section contains an exhibition of lapidary art, for which the Teotihuacans were renowned. Still is obvious in their funerary masks and the figurines fashioned in fine stone.

General view of the last section of the Teotihuacan Hall. On the left is a mural by Nicolás Moreno, it shows the natural habitat on the outskirts of Teotihuacan. Standing in the center is a sculpture of the goddess Chalchiuhtlicue with a photographic mural of the Pyramid of the Sun in the background.

Tripod ceramic vessel of "thin orange ware", adorned with a band of small anthropomorphic figures and a jaguar. (photograph on page 29)

Huehueteotl, the old fire god, was one of the earliest gods on the Central Plateau. The Teotihuacans maintained this tradition to such an extent that it was one of their most frequently represented deities.

Tripod bowl with lid, found as an offering in a Teotihuacan burial.

32

Tripod bowl with lid and adorned with shell disks, a typical form in Teotihuacan ceramics.

It was customary in Teotihuacan to paint the buildings with religious motifs. Mineral colors were used and the paint was applied on top of a stucco base. This is a fragment of a mural.

Above, right: The coloring of this funerary mask of painted earthenware is particularly attractive with earrings and nose ornament, the latter representing a stylized butterfly.

Below, right: Group of vessels for domestic use. Outstanding are enormous jars for storing grain, pots for cooking food, amphoras with three handles used to carry water, and large braziers for burning copal incense.

Above: Scale-model reproduction of a section of the Temple of Quetzalcoatl, from the Citadel at Teotihuacan. The stone buildings were usually covered with stucco and painted in bright colors.

Right: Small earthenware female figurine with a pathological deformation. Traces of its original color remain.

Left: Small male sculpture. Teotihuacan lapidary workers always gave the desired form to hard and semiprecious stones, such as serpentine, alabaster, and quartz.

Right: Funerary mask with turquoise, serpentine, and shell incrustations. This piece stands out among the museum's masterpieces.

Below: Anthropomorphic and zoomorphic miniatures in obsidian, which show the Teotihuacans' technical domination of this type of work.

Above: Representations of local flora and fauna are frequent in the Teotihuacan culture. This miniature jaguar is an example of the realistic style predominating in this kind of small-scale artwork.

Right: The geometric beauty of the enormous water goddess, Chalchiuhtlicue, contrasts with the tiny jaguar. Found in the Plaza of the Moon at Teotihuacan.

Reproduction of the mural found in the Palace of the Plumed Shells at Teotihuacan and located under the Palace of Quetzalpapalotl (Quetzal butterfly), on one side of the Plaza of the Moon.

Toltec Hall

Gigantic stone sculpture known as an *atlante*. It was used to support the beams of the Temple of Tlahuizcal-pantecutli in the city of Tula, Hidalgo, and measures 4.60 m in height. Early Postclassic period.

By around the middle of the eighth century the importance of the City of Teotihuacan had declined rapidly, and with it ended what has been called the Classic Horizon. At this time, the Postclassic period begins, which lasts until the Spanish Conquest. The decline of Teotihuacan did not signify as at times has been said, a step backward for the urban cultures of the Central Plateau, but rather the contrary. Other cities, contemporary to Teotihuacan, such as Xochicalco, in the present-day state of Morelos, and Cholula, in the valley of Puebla, reached their peak at this time. Moreover, groups of Chichimecs arrived in Mesoamerica from the north to found new cities, of which Tula is, without doubt, the most outstanding. It is unlikely that the cities of this period were as large as Teotihuacan, but they must all have been important urban centers.

Often only scant mention is made of the urban planning or the productive activities of the inhabitants of these centers, for little is known about these social aspects. More attention has been devoted to the buildings that form the administrative, religious and political centers of these cities.

This hall should be called the Postclassic period in the Central Plateau, since even though it is mainly dedicated to Tula, reference is also made to other contemporary cities.

The first section is dedicated to Xochicalco, which means "House of Flowers". Sculptures on display include the famous stelae of Xochicalco and the sculpture representing the stylized head of a parakeet or parrot which formed part of the court for the ball game at this city. There are also pieces of ceramics and other objects worked in alabaster, shell, and so on.

A photographic mural illustrates the base of the Temple of the Plumed Serpents.

The second section of the hall is dedicated to Tula. This city was founded by a group of Chichimecs who reached the Central Plateau during the time of the decline of Teotihuacan. The Chichimecs lived side by side with the Teotihuacan population, adopted many aspects of that great culture and called themselves Toltecs, a name that means "artifice" or "artist".

Interesting architectonic and sculptural elements from Tula are on display, such as the serpent columns, the bench decorated with bas-relief, and pillars with warrior figures in which the influence of Teotihuacan is evident. The sculpture of a "chacmool", or reclining figure representing the divine messenger who transported the "sacrificial offering" to the sun, is a typical example of Toltec art, as are the standard bearers, Atlantean figures or warriors. In the center of the hall is the replica of a stone Atlantean sculpture measuring 4.60 meters in height, and made up of four interlocking pieces joined by the mortise and tenon system. This is the piece of sculpture with which the city of Tula is perhaps most closely identified.

Other pieces illustrate the fusion of sculpture and architecture that took place in Tula, as seen in the fragment of stone figures, slabs, and columns decorated with bas-reliefs.

The ceramics from Tula are very crude. The quality of Toltec pottery does not even remotely compare with that of Teotihuacan. By contrast, the plumbate ceramics from Guatemala represent, by virtue of their quality, some of the most highly prized items of trade for this period.

The Toltecs developed irrigation techniques to increase agricultural activity to maintain the growing population of the city. It is certain that tribute received from subjected nations permitted, to a large extent, the enrichment of the city and supplied it with products scarce in that region such as seashells, feathers, greenstone and tropical fruits.

The hall ends with an exhibit of objects from Tenayuca, a city founded around A.D. 1200. There is an architect's model of the Tenayuca pyramid, which dates from the Toltec period and is made up of eight pyramids superimposed on one another. This pyramid's outstanding feature is that the upper part had twin shrines, as did the Great Temple (Templo Mayor) of the Mexicas, and also that it was entirely surrounded by a wall of sculpted serpents.

Stela 3 from Xochicalco, Morelos. It bears the effigy of Quetzalcoatl, who sacrificed himself in Teotihuacan to create the Fifth Sun. It has calendar inscriptions.

The sculptures known by the name of Chac-Mool, semireclining, with the hands on the stomach and the head turned to one side, are characteristic of the Toltec era, but they appeared afterwards in the Maya region and in other parts of the Central Plateau. This figure comes from Tula, Hidalgo, and differs in that the hands are clasped over the stomach instead of holding a vessel, as is usually the case.

Above: Figure made of clay covered with mosaic in mother-of-pearl. It represents the face of a Toltec warrior emerging from the jaws of a coyote.

Left: Small stone *atlante* with the arms raised. It probably supported an altar. It retains the original paint. Found at Tula, Hidalgo. Toltec culture, Early Post-Classic period.

Above: Sculptures of Toltec warriors dressed with their garments and headpieces, holding their arms: *atlatl* and darts. Found at Tula, Hidalgo

Right: Bowl made of *tecalli* (a type of white alabaster) and known as a vessel of sacrifice. It is painted with a descending quetzal, which might be the symbol of the sun, to whom the liquid which it held was dedicated. This piece was found underneath the Temple of the Plumed Serpent at Xochicalco, Morelos.

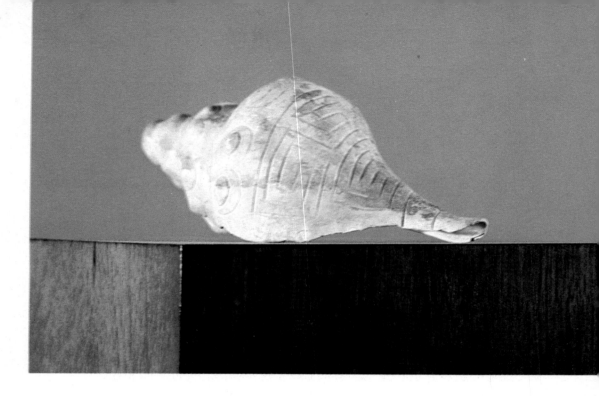

Above: Decorated shell found in the Chamber of the Offerings, in Xochicalco, Morelos. During the pre-Columbian period, it was common to place offerings in special areas of religious buildings.

Right: Stone sculpture of the head of a macaw. This was perhaps a marker in the ball court. Found at Xochicalco, Morelos.

Below: Stone of the Four Glyphs, showing the use of two different traditions to represent the Mesoamerican calendar: the Nahua system and the Maya-Zapotec system.

Left: Zoomorphic bowl made of "plumbate" ceramic ware from Chiapas or Guatemala, but found in the Toltec region. Due to the high quality of manufacture and beautiful polish, these pieces were much prized and one of the most important articles for commercial exchange.

Right: Figure of polychrome earthenware used as a propitiatory offering in the shrines constructed especially for the worship of Tlaloc, god of rain. Toltec culture, Early Post-Classic period.

Mexica Hall

The most important hall of the museum is reserved for the Mexica culture. Located in the center of the museum. Its grand dimensions were designed to amply frame the culture of this people.

The Mexicas, also known as the Aztecs, founded the city of Tenochtitlan in 1325. When the Spaniards arrived two centuries later the Mexicas controlled the most powerful empire in Mesoamerica. A warlike and conquering people par excellence, the Mexicas managed to subjugate, either directly or by means of commercial activity, nations as distant as the Huastecs from the Gulf Coast of Mexico and the Zapotecs and Mixtecs of Oaxaca. They also concentrated tribute from the most distant and varied

The *Ocelotl-Cuauhxicalli* (Jaguar-eagle) is a stone vessel in the form of a jaguar. It served as a depository for the hearts of human victims sacrificed to Huitzilopochtli and Tezcatlipoca. It is 94 cm high and belongs to the Mexica culture of the fourteenth to sixteenth centuries A.D. From Tenochtitlan.

regions in their great capital, Tenochtitlan. Many of these subjected peoples were the first to ally themselves with the Spaniards to overthrow the Mexica empire.

The Mexica hall is divided into various sections. Sculptures of great beauty such as the head of the Eagle Knight and the monumental Cuauhxicalli grace the entrance landing. The central portion houses an extraordinary selection of other large sculptures dominated by the Sun Stone (Aztec Calendar). One can find here the statue of Coatlicue (earth goddess and mother of Huitzilopochtli, patron god of the Mexicas, and Coyolxauhqui), the Cihuateteo (goddess of women who died in childbirth), the Tzompantli or wall of skulls, Coyolxauhqui (moon goddess and sister of Huitzilopochtli).

On the right side of the hall is a section dedicated to a physical description of the Mexica people, followed by a history of the long pilgrimage undertaken from their place of origin to the founding of Tenochtitlan. One of the great Aztec monoliths, the Stone of Tizoc, also narrates part of Mexica history after the founding of this city.

Next is a section dedicated to the city of Mexico-Tenochtitlan, showing plans and reproductions of various architectural elements and adornments used in Aztec building. A mural of the city as it doubtlessly appeared on the arrival of the Spaniards is shown, together with an architect's model of the great ceremonial center including the impressive Great Temple with its twin shrines dedicated to the gods Huitzilopochtli and Tlaloc, and the round temple of Quetzalcoatl (as wind god), among other buildings. The entire sacred precinct was encircled by a great wall.

In the back of the hall is an exhibition of documents and drawings on the Mexica economy, from its beginnings to the establishment of a system of tribute that provided the Aztec empire with its main source of wealth. There is also an extremely realistic diorama which shows the variety of products found in the marketplace of Tlatelolco, the most important in the empire.

The section to the left is dedicated to Aztec religion, with representations of the wind, earth, life and death deities, among others. There are also other sculptures connected with religion, such as ceremonial receptacles and solar disks. A showcase contains different objects utilized in human sacrifice; these include the stone on which the victim was stretched in order that his heart be removed, sacrificial knives, and others.

Another section is dedicated to smaller sculptures worked in stone. Notable are the coiled serpents. At the end of the hall we find examples of Aztec ceramic ware: vases, plates, masks, incense holders, stamps, anthropomorphic vessels, and the like. Fine stoneworking techniques are demonstrated in an obsidian vase in the form of a monkey, as well as in a beautiful diorite squash.

Also displayed are samples of Aztec jewelry, made of bone, rock crystal, gold, wood, seashells and obsidian, among other materials.

There is a rich variety of musical instruments: flutes, whistles, trumpets, drums and instruments made from seashells and tortoise shell, as well as wooden drums beautifully decorated in bas-relief. This part of the Mexica hall ends with the display of pieces representative of the fall of the Aztec empire to the Spaniards and show the introduction of elements from the new culture.

Right: Sculpture of Coatlicue, goddess of the earth and of death, represented as a decapitated woman from whose neck spring two serpent heads, which symbolize streams of blood. She wears a necklace of hands and hearts, while her own hands are serpent heads and her feet eagle claws. The sculpture measures 2.57 meters high, comes from Tenochtitlan, and dates from A.D. 1250 - 1321.

The obsidian monkey is one of the museum's most valuable pieces. Made of a highly polished piece of obsidian (volcanic glass), it represents the god of dance, play, and love. This piece comes from Texcoco, state of Mexico.

Ceremonial brazier inspired by the leaves of the maguey (agave) and by the thorns of the plant. Found in the marketplace of Tlatelolco, Mexico City.

Above and below: The monolith known as the Stone of Tizoc. It shows the victories attributed to Tizoc, the seventh *tlatoani* (sovereign) of the Mexicas (1481-1486). This round monolith in trachyte was found in the Zócalo, or main plaza, in Mexico City and was probably a votive monument dedicated to the sun.

Above: Sculpture with incrustations in the eyes and teeth, which accentuate the realism of the work. It represents a common man and is to be found in the right-hand corner of the hall, where other sculptures represent Mcxica types: men, women, and old men.

Left: Sculpture of a Mexica noble, attired in the robes appropiate to his rank.

Left: Sculpture of a *teocalli,* or temple. It depicts myths governing ceremonial combat.

Below: The Stone of the Warriors, which held the maguey thorns used by warriors in rites of autosacrifice. They perforated their earlobes to draw blood as offerings.

The *Tzompantli*, or altar of skulls, 93 cm high, is a monument dedicated to the sun. It was found in the precinct of the Great Temple *(Templo Mayor)* of Tenochtitlan (14th -16th centuries A.D.) The *Xiuh-molpilli* was made of 52 reeds, symbolizing a 52-year cycle. The bundle represented the period of time that had just "died" or been completed. As a symbolic corpse it was placed in the central cavity of the altar.

Above and below: Diorama of the most important market in central Mexico. It was located in Tlatelolco, the ancient city incorporated into Tenochtitlan in 1473. Cacao beans served as currency, but most of the transactions were made in kind.

The Sun Stone, also known as the Aztec Calendar Stone, is probably the best-known monument of the Mexica. It was, in fact, a sculpture dedicated to the sun and was never really a calendar. An olivine basalt monolith 3.57 meters in diameter and weighing 24.5 tons. It was sculpted during the reign of Axayacatl, sixth *tlatoani* (emperor or king) of the Aztecs in the year 13 *acatl* (13 reed, 1479), and was placed on the Great Temple *(Templo Mayor)*. With the destruction of the images of the Mexica gods, the sun stone was left in the main square and was later buried by order of the Spanish religious authorities. In 1790 it was discovered and moved to one side of the western tower of the cathedral, where it remained until 1885, when it was transported to the old National Museum of Anthropology.

A mural painted by Luis Covarrubias of Tenochtitlan in the middle of the lake can be seen in the upper part of the hall. Below is an architect's model of the sacred precinct, the religious and political center of the capital, which had a surface area of 520 square meters. Within the sacred precinct of Tenochtitlan was the Great Temple *(Templo Mayor),* topped by twin shrines dedicated to the gods Tlaloc and Huitzilopochtli. Also located here were the temples of Tezcatlipoca and Quetzalcoatl, palaces, pools, ball courts, and trees, all of which were surrounded by a wall with openings permitting access at four places.

Right: Xochipilli, "prince of the flowers", was the god of song, poetry, theater, love, dance, vegetation, and spring. Seated on a throne decorated with flowers and butterflies, he wears jade ear plugs, a collar, and sandals of jaguar skin.

Above: Chac-Mool, carrying on its stomach a disk decorated with symbols.

Below: In the human sacrifice showcase, objects are shown associated with these important religious practices. This is a knife with a mother-of-pearl handle and decorated with a warrior figure.

Wooden drum, *(huehuetl),* from Tenango, state of Mexico. On the upper part, above a thick cord, are the figures of an eagle and a vulture in combat.

"She of the face painted with rattles", Coyolxauhqui, goddess of the moon, sister of Huitzilopochtli (god of war). Both were children of Coatlicue, Coyolxauhqui has rattles painted on her face, *(coyolli* signifies rattles in Nahuatl; *Xauhqui* means she who paints herself). Diorite, 14th - 16th centuries A.D., Tenochtitlan.

Oaxaca Hall

Stone representing a richly attired personage with a headdress ending in long feathers. Mixtec culture, Oaxaca. From Tilantongo, Oaxaca.

In the vast region that runs from the eastern ranges of the Sierra Madre, as far as the Pacific coast, and south to the Isthmus of Tehuantepec, in what is today the state of Oaxaca, flourished two great cultures: the Zapotec and the Mixtec.

The Zapotec culture was the most ancient. Its origins date to the Early Classic period, and it is contemporary with the Olmecs on the Gulf Coast, with whom some kind of relationship must have been maintained in view of the similarities in many cultural elements. The Zapotec people populated mainly the central valleys, and their most important city was Monte Albán. The unique thing about this city is that its administrative and religious center, the palaces of its priests and of its rulers, were built on a mountaintop that had been leveled to provide an enormous plaza surrounded by platforms for temples and other buildings.

Due to its importance, Monte Albán has been used to date the Zapotec culture, and its development is divided into four periods chiefly in accordance with the types of ceramic ware dominant in each phase: Monte Albán I (800 - 300 B.C.), which would correspond to the Upper Preclassic period in the Central Plateau; Monte Albán II (300 - A.D. 100); Monte Albán III (A.D. 100 - 800), which would correspond to the Classic Horizon; and Monte Albán IV and V (A.D. 800 - 1321), the Postclassic Horizon.

The Mixtecs inhabited the mountain ranges of Oaxaca. During the period that saw the decline of Zapotec power, after Monte Albán III, the Mixtecs occupied the central valleys, coexisted with the Zapotec population, and gradually overpowered important cities but without destroying the extant culture. For this reason, Zapotec and Mixtec speaking groups coexist in this region, both preserving their own cultural traditions.

The Mixtecs also built important cities such as Mitla and developed an architectural style characterized by stone buildings with flat roofs or false arch ceilings, and decorated with friezes in geometric designs made with small blocks of stone assembled one next to the other.

Entering from the right, the first part of the hall is dedicated to an exhibition of the Zapotec culture. Near the entrance is a reproduction of the stones known as "The Dancers," belonging to the earliest period of Monte Albán. These were found integrated into the platform of a Monte Albán temple. There are other interesting sculptures in this section, but the most important and varied are the ceramic pieces.

The Zapotecs were excellent ceramicists, and they produced every type of pottery, ranging from simple bowls to elaborate anthropomorphic or zoomorphic urns in a variety of colors. Among the outstanding pieces in this hall are the polychrome ceramic figure known as the Great Jaguar and also the Goddess "13 Serpent."

The cult of the dead attained great importance, and burials were usually accompanied by multiple offerings of jewelry and ceramic ware. Many of the pieces exhibited in this hall come from tombs. There is also a reconstruction of Tomb 104 at Monte Albán, in which one can observe the arrangement of the offerings and Zapotec funerary architecture during the period of their greatest splendor.

Also displayed in this part of the hall are some works in stone such as the door jamb from Las Margaritas and the Stela from Río Grande.

In the garden adjacent to the hall is a complete reconstruction of Tomb 7 from Monte Albán, considered one of the richest in Mesoamerica. In this tomb, lavish Mixtec offerings were found.

Examples of gold and silver work, found in the section dedicated to the Mixtec culture demonstrate one of the arts at which this people excelled. Beautiful items in gold, silver, rock crystal and turquoise are displayed.

The Mixtecs were also distinguished as painters of codices, and have left a valuable legacy to instruct us about their history and their culture. Their ceramic were characterized by a variety of forms, by zoomorphic and anthropomorphic bowls, tripod vases and jars, which at times were decorated with an effigy of the skeleton associated with the god of death. However, the most distinctive trait of these ceramics is the polychrome decoration in the style of the codices.

Stela from Río Grande, representing a personage with arms crossed, with a headdress in the form of a jaguar. From Río Grande, Oaxaca.

Above: General view of the Oaxaca Hall.

Left: Urn with a representation of a deity with a buccal mask in the form of a wide beak. From the Temple of 7 Deer at Monte Albán, Oaxaca.

The Zapotecs were outstanding workers of semiprecious stones. This necklace combines stones cut in the form of beads and is also decorated with marine elements.

Left: Scale model of Tomb 104 at Monte Albán, Oaxaca. Important persons were buried in luxurious tombs with painted walls and a great variety of offerings.

Right: A reproduction of one of the stones with reliefs of men who appear to be dancers. This stone decorates the base of the Temple of the Dancers at Monte Albán, Oaxaca.

Right:Head of Life and Death, made of clay. This is a piece of great representative value, because the right side expresses life, and the left side, which is completely fleshless, signifies death. Thus is shown the duality of life and death.

Above: Influences from Guatemala or Chiapas that reached Oaxaca around 300 B.C. define Monte Albán II. During this period, magnificent earthenware figures were made, such as the one seen here.

Right: Urn with the figure of the Old God 5-F. The headdress ends in a zoomorphic head from which two pieces of material emerge. From Tomb 1 at Loma Larga, Oaxaca.

Above: Polychrome bowl with a hummingbird poised on its edge –a lovely example of Mixtec art. From Tomb 2 at Zaachila, Oaxaca.

Left: Earthenware sculpture known as the Great Jaguar. It belongs to the Zapotec culture, Monte Albán, Oaxaca.

Above: Mixtec jewelry demonstrates high technical ability as well as artistic sensitivity. Different techniques were used to make breastplates, necklaces, rings, and other objects, which are outstanding for the quality of their workmanship. This breastplate, in the form of a shield (*chimalli*) pierced by a group of arrows, comes from Yanhuitlan, Oaxaca.

Right: Polychrome bowl decorated with a skull. Mixtec culture.

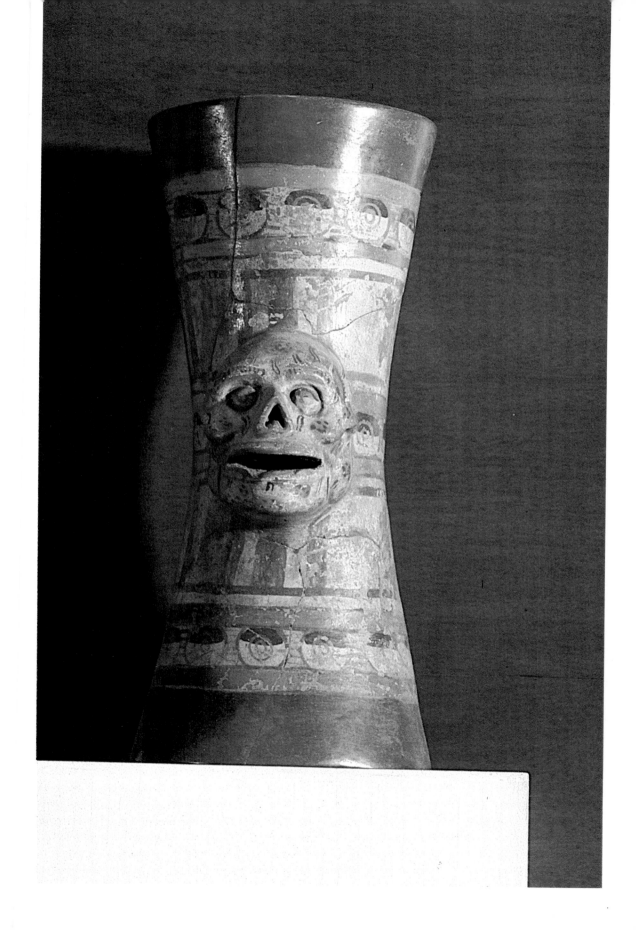

Anthropomorphic polychrome bowl. The adornments and decoration around the mouth are note-worthy. From Zaachila, Oaxaca, Mixtec culture.

Left: Skull in poly-
chrome ceramic ware.
Oaxaca, Mixtec cul-
ture.

Below: Tripod bowl
with polychrome
decoration in the style
of the codices.
Oaxaca, Mixtec cul-
ture.

Mixtec bowl with codex-type decoration. Oaxaca, Mixtec culture.

Gulf of Mexico Hall

Mask with Olmec features found outside the Gulf Coast area. It is believed that the presence of these objects, far from their place of origin, was due to a diffusion of this culture throughout much of Mesoamerica.

During the pre-Columbian period, the coasts of the Gulf of Mexico and the adjacent regions housed three great cultures: the Olmec in the state of Tabasco and the southern portion of the state of Veracruz: the Totonac, in the center of Veracruz; and the Huastec, which extended from the Soto la Marina River in Tamaulipas to the Cazones River in Veracruz, to the northeast of Querétaro, southeast of San Luis Potosí and to the south of Tamaulipas.

The Olmec culture was the earliest of the strongly stratified or class societies of Mesoamerica. It reached its height in the Preclassic period, between 1200 and 600 B.C. The influence of the Olmec was so widespread throughout Mesoamerica that it is considered the "mother" culture from which others derived. However, all of the elements characteristic of Olmec culture have not been found together at any of the archaeological sites outside of the coastal region, which suggests that the presence of Olmec traits in other parts of Mesoamerica was due to the commercial influence they exercised, rather than to a military conquest.

Monumental pieces of sculpture, such as the colossal heads, are typical of this culture. A high degree of realism is combined with an abstract conception of volume, skillfully handled. One can admire this combination of anatomical detail and sculptural synthesis in the figure known as the Wrestler.

The small sculptures in lapidary stone, the celts, and the articles of personal adornment are also worth noting, as are the ceramic bowls and figurines of entire bodies, faces, or masks. Elongated skulls, resulting from cranial deformation, and the corners of the mouths depicted in feline style with the lips curled downward, are typical of the Olmec artistic style.

The culture from the center of Veracruz occupies the second section of this hall. This culture reached its height during the Classic period, between A.D. 200 and 800. It is characterized by earthenware figures and smiling faces and by the famous toys with wheels. The stone yokes, *palmas* (palmate-shaped objects, probably held in place by the belt), *hachas* (slab-shaped objects, probably held in place by the belt), rails (eccentric-shaped stone sculpture), and padlocks constitute the typical sculptural complex of central Veracruz. The precise use of these objects is unknown, but it is believed that they are connected with the cult of the dead and with the ball game.

Some reproductions to scale of architecture are also exhibited in this part of the hall, such as buildings of Cempoala, and the Pyramid of the Niches at El Tajín, both sites in Veracruz.

Objects belonging to the Huastec culture are shown in the third and last section. The ceramic ware is noted for the fineness of the clay, which was covered by a polished white slip that enhanced the delicacy of its form. This type of pottery later became polychrome with brown, black, and red decorations on the same white or cream background. The sculptures in stone are also outstanding. The body of the Huastec youth in the center of the hall is covered with inscriptions. But perhaps the most singular talent of the Huastecs is revealed by their work in shell and bone, in which they were possibly the most outstanding artists in Mesoamerica.

Many aspects of the ideology, religion, and scientific knowledge of the Huastecs are unknown. We do know, however, that one of their principal gods was Quetzalcoatl, and during the period in which the Aztecs extended their domain to this region, Huastec influence was felt both in religion and in the use of the calendar. In turn, the Huastecs received influences from the cultures of central Veracruz and of the Mixtec area, the latter of which manifested itself in the polychrome pottery.

Other important deities represented in this hall include Xilonen (Aztec corn goddess), Mictlantecuhtli (the god of death), and female figures probably connected with fertility, as well as sculptures of old men connected with fire and with the sun, which impregnates the earth.

Stone relief that represents a priest with a jaguar helmet and surrounded by an enormous rattlesnake.

Above: The sculpted stone monuments of the Olmecs of the Gulf Coast demonstrate an interest in realism and anatomical detail. Colossal head from the Preclassic period, from San Lorenzo, Veracruz.

Right: Colossal head number 6 from San Lorenzo, Veracruz. The monumental heads are the most famous Olmec sculptures.

Right: Despite the bad condition in which these figurines from San Lorenzo, Veracruz, were found, their high quality can be recognized. They give an idea of the physical type of the people in that region.

Below: Stone sculpture known as the Olmec Wrestler, from the Upper Preclassic period.

Right: The physical appearance of the Olmecs combined with the typical characteristics of the Olmec artistic style, is portrayed in ceramic figurines. Here we see a stout personage with skull deformation and a mouth with lips curling downward, jaguar style.

Left: Head of an Olmec figurine made of stone. From the Gulf Coast, but found in the state of Mexico.

Left: Greenstone figurine that formed part of a large offering of objects made of this material. Found at Cerro de las Mesas, Veracruz.

Right: Ceremonial brazier of polychrome clay with the effigy of Tlaloc, god of rain, 1.50 m in height, 1.62 m in circumference. From the Totonac culture of Central Veracruz.

Left: Stela representing Quetzalcoatl, one of the most important gods of the Huastec culture. From Castillo de Teayo, Veracruz.

Below: Male figure with moveable arms. Excellent example of a smiling face. From Central Veracruz.

Above: The potters of Central Veracruz created figures of great realism, outstanding among which are the so-called smiling faces.

Left: Sculpture known as the Huastec Youth, representing a naked adolescent with cranial deformation and with a hand on the chest. The entire body is covered with bas-reliefs. From Tamuín, San Luis Potosí.

Right: Votive celt made of stone, 27 cm in height. Classic period, from Central Veracruz.

Right: This sculpted yoke together with other artifacts connected with the ball game and the cult of the dead, such as axes, padlocks, eccentricly shaped rails, and palmate stones, make up the sculptural complex typical of Central Veracruz.

Left: Palmate stone sculpture of a lizard, belonging to the ball game-related sculptural complex of Central Veracruz.

Right and below: The Huastecs not only utilized their artistic abilities to work seashells, but also fashioned bone into true works of art. There are personal adornments of great delicacy and aesthetic value.

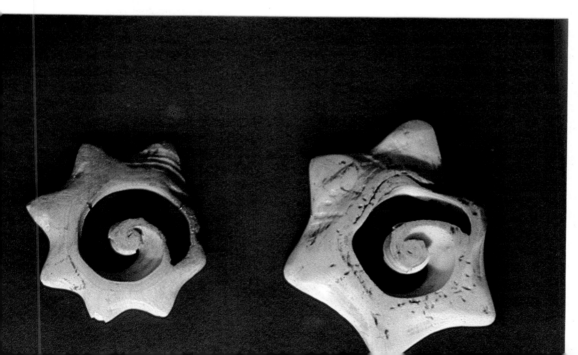

Sculpture of the Mexica goddess Xilonen, which is a typical example of the influence exerted by the Mexicas in the Huastec region at the time of the Conquest. Found at Castillo de Teayo, Veracruz.

Maya Hall

The Mayas maintained a certain common identity by means of language and some basic characteristics with which they are culturally identified, despite the extensive and varied area that they inhabited and their long history, which dates from the Early Preclassic period until the arrival of the Spaniards.

The Mayas occupied the southern part of Mesoamerica, from the Grijalva River in the state of Tabasco, Mexico, to the present-day republics of Honduras, El Salvador, Guatemala, and Belize in Central America. They had to deal with the dryness of the land in the north of the Yucatan Peninsula, with the swamps of Tabasco, the tropical forests of Guatemala, Belize, Chiapas, and Campeche, and with the highlands and mountains of Guatemala and Chiapas.

This wide territory can be divided into three great natural zones: south, central, and north. Each area appears to have reached its zenith at a different time. The southern and essentially mountainous region was the first, as can be seen at sites such as Takalik, Chocolá, and others in the highlands of Guatemala. In the central region, located on low-lying land watered by abundant rivers, great cities, such as Tikal in the Guatemalan Petén, Uaxactún in Honduras, and Bonampak and Palenque in Chiapas, flourished during the Classic period.

Although the north of the Yucatán Peninsula had been occupied from the Preclassic period, it was not until the tenth and eleventh centuries of our era, when the Maya cities in the central region had been practically abandoned, that numerous centers arose in this region. These are known today as Hochob, Edzná, Kabah, Uxmal, Labná, Chichén Itzá, Mayapán, Izamal, Tulum, and many more, both inland and along the coast.

At the entrance to the hall is an architect's model in relief showing the areas occupied by the Maya culture, together with photographs and a mural that illustrate the characteristics of the natural habitat.

On the right-hand side is an area dedicated mainly to ceramic ware and other aspects of Classic period Maya culture, such as music, the system of numerical notation, and religion. The collection of figurines from the island of Jaina, Campeche, is of outstanding beauty, as are the polychrome vases and plates.

Larger sculptures, such as the stelae and stucco friezes, are to be found in a large hall that also houses architects' models of the religious-administrative centers of cities important during the Classic period.

A staircase leads from the center of the hall to a lower level, where one can see exhibits of funerary customs as well as a reconstruction of the Royal Tomb of Palenque. In the garden outside the main hall is a replica of Building II at Hochob, Campeche, together with other buildings containing lifesize reconstructions of the Bonampak murals. There are also stelae and sculptures from various parts of Mexico and Central America in these gardens.

The left-hand section of the hall is dedicated to the exhibition of articles from the Postclassic period in the Yucatan Peninsula. Relations at this period between the Mayas and the inhabitants of the Central Plateau were evidenced in various ways, such as the Toltec style of the Chac-Mool of Chichén Itzá which is to be found here. Apart from this sculpture, there are numerous examples of ceramics made of materials such as Plumbate and fine orange; of metallurgy and lapidary art; and with reproductions of mural painting.

Large mask representing a solar deity, Kinich Ahau, with a jaguar (the earth) on the lower part and a bird serving as headdress in the upper. (photograph on page 101)

Stela number 18 from Yaxchilán, Chiapas, represents a ruler who has captured a person named Chuén, shown bowing his head in the lower portion. Late Classic period, eighth century A.D.

Left: These small sculptures modeled in clay are known as Jaina figurines, from their origin in the island of this name off the coast of Campeche. This one represents a priest surrounded by a kind of altar with serpent heads at the sides and bunches of feathers at the top. Late Classic period, A.D. 600 - 900.

Right: A Jaina figurine representing a woman of rank, with a fine cotton *huipil*, elaborate hairstyle, and facial decoration consisting of scarring on the chin and between the eyebrows.

Left: Lintel number 53 from Yaxchilán, Chiapas, represents a ruler and a woman holding a bundle, which may indicate that they are carring out an important transaction. Late Classic period, eighth century A.D.

Above: Polychrome plate decorated with a hunting scene. The outer band contains the hunters disguised as deer: in the center is a hunter with a trapped stag. From Jaina, Campeche. Late Classic period, A.D. 600 - 900.

Right: Polychrome ceremonial urn with the effigy of Chaac, "he of the long nose", god of rain. From Mayapan, Yucatan. Late Postclassic period, A.D. 1250 - 1521.

Left: A well-known sculpture of the head of a young male personage, found as part of the offerings in the secret tomb of the Temple of the Inscriptions in Palenque, Chiapas, Late Classic period, A.D. 600 - 900.

Right: Reconstruction of the secret tomb found in the interior of the pyramid of the Temple of the Inscriptions in Palenque, Chiapas. The funerary chamber, 9 meters in length by 4 meters high, contains the sarcophagous where the body of a royal personage was deposited with rich offerings. Late Classic period, A.D. 600 - 900.

Bas-relief in stone, known as the Cross of Palenque, found in the temple of the same name. The central motif is a cross symbolizing the sacred ceiba tree or the deified maize plant, which provided the first food for humanity. At the side are two personages of different sizes, the larger of which appears to be offering an image of a small, large-nosed god to the cross. Late Classic period, A.D. 600 - 900.

Stucco sculpture of a masculine face with typically Maya physical characteristics: wide face, pronounced fold in the eyelid, giving the eyes an almond shape, and well defined lips. It is probably a portrait. Found in Palenque, Chiapas, Late Classic period, A.D. 600 - 900.

Right: Lintel number 43 from Yaxchilán, Chiapas. This represents a ruler of the jaguar lineage. He holds a scepter, symbol of his high rank. Facing him is a woman also of high rank, attired in a beautiful *huipil*. She offers him the cord for autosacrifice. Late Classic period, A.D. 772.

Below: Greenstone plaque 9 cm in length, with the figure of a personage in openwork and incised bas-relief. Late Classic period, A.D. 600 - 900.

The Jaina figurines show a remarkable variety of dress and adornments, both feminine and masculine. In some cases it is easy to identify the activity of the person represented, so these figures provide valuable information on social differentiation. Right: Person wearing a long robe, with short sleeves and a high, wide-brimmed hat. Below: Warrior with a feather costume that covers the entire body and a shield. Jaina, Campeche.

Right: Ceremonial urn with a human figure with a removable head. He sits on the edge of the bowl with elbows resting on knees. On the front of the bowl is a decoration in the form of a bird mask, with the beak framing a human head with ear plugs and nose ornament in the form of a claw. From Chinkultic, Chiapas. Late Classic period, A.D. 600 - 900.

Right: The human figure was one of the most frequently utilized motifs in ceramic decoration of the Late Classic period, as can be seen in this polychrome vase found at Atitlán, Guatemala.

Below: Reconstruction of the Chenesstyle Temple II at Hochob, state of Campeche. The façade is decorated with an enormous mask, the mouth of which forms the entrance to the building's interior. Classic period.

Right: Sculpture widely known as the Queen of Uxmal. This formed part of the façade of a substructure of the Magician's Pyramid in Uxmal, Yucatán. Late Classic period, A.D. 600 - 900.

Large mask made in the stone mosaic technique, representing the face of Chaac, god of rain. This mask originally formed part of the decoration of the facade of the Codz-Pop, the main temple at Kabah, Yucatan. Late Classic period.

Northern Mexico Hall

The ceramic ware of Casas Grandes, Chihuahua, has an unmistakable personality and beauty. The colors are mixed in multiple geometric designs to which at times are added zoomorphic or anthropomorphic forms.

Northern Mexico refers to the extensive region that today includes the Mexican states of Guanajuato, San Luis Potosí, Durango, Zacatecas, Aguascalientes, Tamaulipas, Nuevo León, Coahuila, Chihuahua, and Sonora, and the southern part of the United States. The ecological conditions were not, generally speaking, favorable to agriculture with the techniques available in the pre-Columbian era; therefore, there was neither the population density nor the urban development that existed in Mesoamerica.

The culture of the peoples who inhabited these areas, as shown in this hall, has been classified into three great types: the Desert and Plains cultures, the cultures of Marginal Mesoamerica, and the Oasis cultures.

In the Desert region, where agriculture was impossible, the inhabitants dedicated themselves to hunting and gathering from very early times (10,000 B. C.). When the large mammals died out around 5,000 B.C., some groups specialized in the collection of wild plants, while others continued hunting bison (above all, on the plains of the United States). But generally speaking, they took advantage of all resources offered by their natural habitat. They had to move constantly to find food and thus were never able to form large political units, nor did the population increase. These cultures changed little from prehistoric times until the Spanish Conquest and, even after the Conquest, were the last to submit to colonialization.

But the influence of the agricultural people of Mesoamerica was felt in all those places where the natural habitat allowed for agricultural development. A strip of land from the states of Guanajuato, San Luis Potosí, Querétaro, Durango, and Zacatecas is known as marginal Mesoamerica because, during a period of greater humidity prior to around A.D. 1000, some groups established themselves in sedentary settlements and developed an agriculture complemented by hunting and gathering. With the encroaching desert, however, these people emigrated, probably south.

From the beginning of our era both in the southern United States and in northern Mexico, a culture appeared in some areas that has been called the Oasis culture. These groups from the north were receivers of many aspects of Mesoamerican cultures: they were acquainted with agriculture, founded urban centers of reasonable importance, and produced ceramics, textiles, etc. However, because of their isolation, their culture developed distinctive traits. Some groups from the north of Sonora and Chihuahua belong to this tradition.

In the first part of the hall are utensils, adornments, and objects connected with the funerary practices and religious beliefs of the hunter-gatherer peoples. Rock paintings formed one of the most outstanding artistic expressions of these peoples.

Characteristic materials of the cultures of marginal Mesoamerica include ceramics with so-called cloisonné decoration, polychrome bowls and jars, clay or stone pipes, as well as some stone sculptures.

The most outstanding expression of the Oasis cultures has been found at sites dating from after A.D. 1000, such as at Casas Grandes. The polychrome ceramic ware with geometric designs is noteworthy, as are the adornments made of copper, shell, bone, turquoise mosaic, and greenstone. Urbanization of this area was totally different from that of Mesoamerica, as can be seen from an architect's model of multistoried dwelling houses.

Right: The inhabitants of Casas Grandes, Chihuahua, were excellent lapidary workers and made objects that were both ornamental and functional.

Above: Model of a section of Casas Grandes, Chihuahua. These houses of several stories and numerous rooms marked a period of great urban development. They were made of adobe and beams, with the doors in the form of a "T."

Below: The craftsmen of Casas Grandes, Chihuahua, attained a high degree of skill in metal work, as can be seen in this small tortoise.

Western Mexico Hall

The present-day states of Sinaloa, Nayarit, Jalisco, Colima, Michoacán, and Guerrero contain the geographical area known as Western Mexico.

After A.D. 600. Western Mexico shared more cultural traits with Mesoamerica than in earlier phases. In general, however, this region remained distinct, because there were no great urban centers except, at a very late date, for Tarascan settlements.

The earliest cultures of Western Mexico belonged to the Preclassic Horizon (1200 B.C. - A.D. 200). Ceramic ware found at El Opeño, Michoacán, and at Chupícuaro, Guanajuato, included bowls, figurines of various types, and personal adornments that formed part of the funerary offerings.

During the Classic Horizon in Mesoamerica in the West, those groups living in Sinaloa, Nayarit, Jalisco, Colima, and Guerrero managed to produce a ceramic ware of extraordinary quality, with styles characteristic of each place. Large and elegant hollow figures are typical of this period, as are innumerable small figurines, which have provided valuable sociological information through their representation of numerous activities and varying styles of dress, adornment, and customs.

Important ceremonial centers began to appear at this time, and there are traces of agricultural development, would have permitted a higher degree of urbanization.

Typical of this period in Jalisco, Colima, and Nayarit are the shaft tombs, underground chambers entered through a shaft, in which offerings of anthropomorphic ceramic ware were placed.

In Colima, outstanding workmanship was shown in the manufacture of a highly polished red and brown ceramic ware. The makers of this ware possessed unlimited imagination, leaving behind them reproductions in clay of varied human types and poses, and of local fauna and vegetables.

Another type of ceramic ware that probably originated in the West was that decorated with the cloisonné technique, which consists of designs formed by different-colored strips of clay that were affixed to the bowl with *copal* or another resin.

In the ceramics of Jalisco, Colima, and Nayarit from the Classic Theocratic period (A.D. 200 - 800), there are frequent representations of deformed human beings, such as individuals suffering from dropsy, with lips parted vertically rather than horizontally, etc. It is probable that these representations were related to magico-religious concepts.

In Guerrero, the Mezcala River region is distinguished for its lapidary techniques. Masks, amulets, and celts were made from very dense stone that was locally available. However, the most unique lapidary object types were reproductions of miniature temples.

The first sections of the hall display different styles of West Mexican ceramics, ranging from Chupícuaro and El Opeño figurines to figurines from the Classic period. In the last part of the hall are representative pieces of the Tarascan culture, which flourished during the Postclassic Horizon in the central region of Michoacán. Over the course of time, the Tarascan dominion achieved the status of an empire that dominated a wide area of the West. Although contemporary with the Mexicas, the Tarascans always maintained their independence.

The Tarascans made magnificent ceramics and lapidary objects and were outstanding especially in the art of metalworking. With the Mixtecs, they were the first to use metals such as copper, gold, and silver to make ornaments and utensils and to use the repoussé and lost wax techniques.

At the end of the hall is an architect's model of the ceremonial center of the Tarascan capital Tzintzuntzan, Michoacán, in which the singular design of the semicircular platforms can be appreciated. Tzintzuntzan is located on the shores of Lake Pátzcuaro and was probably the most important city of western Mesoamerica.

Kneeling woman. The figures from Jalisco are made of a highly polished earthenware. At times, part of the body is painted red and has a geometric design in black to indicate body painting, as in this example. (photograph on page 121)

The ceramic figurines of San Jerónimo, Guerrero, show a marked disproportion between the size of the head and the remainder of the body. Preclassic period, 800-200 B.C.

Above: In the foreground, the Chac–Mool of Ihuatzio, Michoacán. In the background, a mural painted by Pablo O'Higgins.

Right: Male clay figure from Jalisco. As is frecuently the case with these figures, it has an elongated head, a large and pronounced nose, and the eyes are represented by small balls of clay.

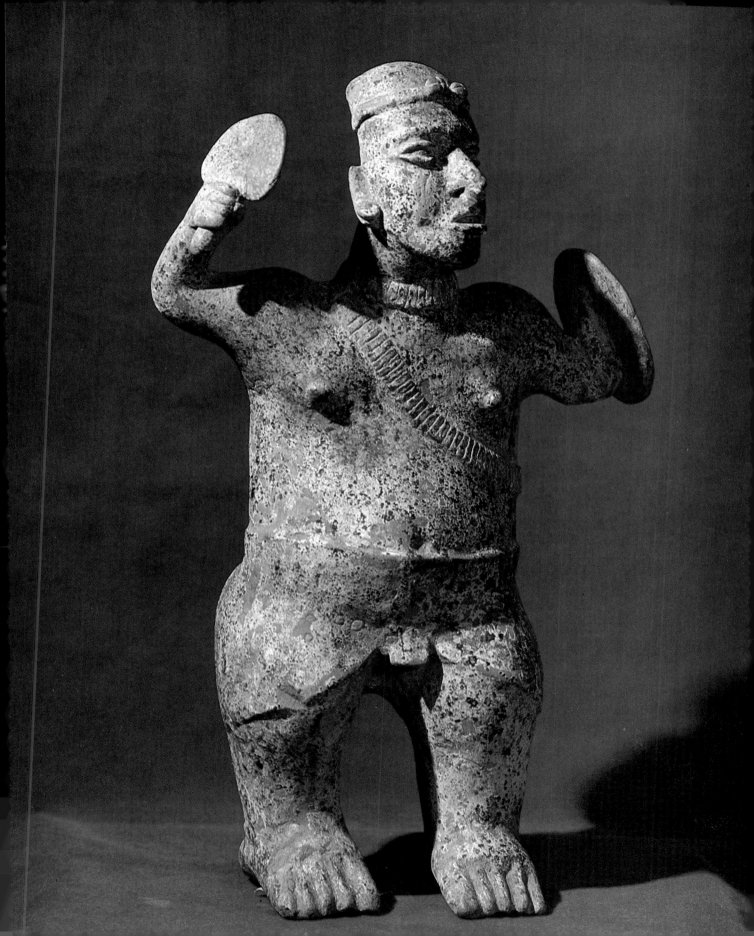

Above: The peoples of Western Mexico were very fond of personal adornment. They combined the various materials within their reach, such as greenstone, turquoise, rock crystal, and shell with excellent taste.

Right: Polychrome bowl with cloisonné-style decoration (detail above). This technique consists of making the design in colored strips, which are then attached to the bowl with an adhesive (copal or another resin). Later these pieces are cut following the design, and the cut parts are filled with clay of other colors to make the design stand out. This type of ceramic ware is more frequently found in Western Mexico, and is therefore thought to have originated there.

During the Classic period, the potters of Colima were noted for their manufacture of highly polished red or brown ceramics. The human figures are highly realistic in form and expression. To date, this type of pottery has only appeared in tombs, and is therefore thought to be for funerary use.

Above: Some objects, such as this ear plug found in Western Mexico, may be the products of commerce with other regions of Mesoamerica.

Left: The potters of Colima represented the fauna of the region in earthenware.

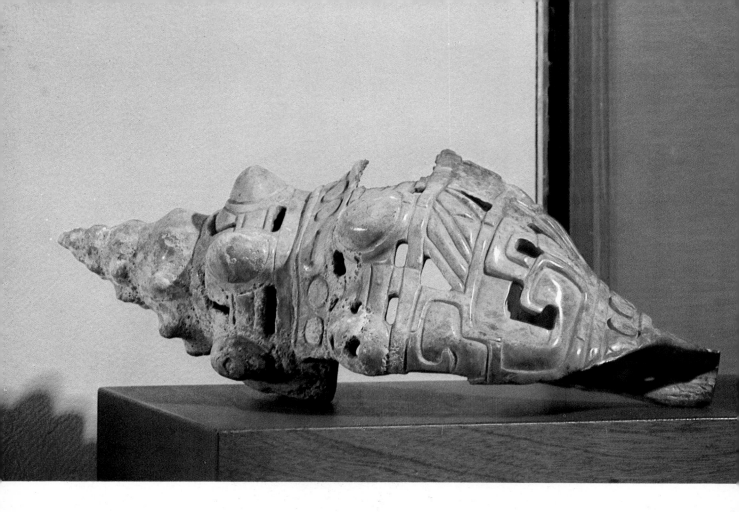

The Tarascan people fashioned materials such as greenstone, turquoise, rock crystal, metals, and shells into adornments. This shell (above) and the rock crystal ear plug with turquoise mosaic (right), are from the area surrounding Apatzingán, Michoacán.

Ethnography Halls

Detail of a traditional woman's dress from the group of costumes to be found in the Introduction to Ethnography Hall.

Nearly 3 million indigenous people, belonging to groups that still retain some traces of their pre-Columbian ancestors, are now distributed throughout the 25 states of the Mexican Republic.

The majority of the indigenous villages and hamlets form the large rural population of the central and southern parts of the country, as well as the small communities scattered throughout the mountains to the north and in the desert regions of Mexico's northwest. These ethnic groups occupy part of the territory that formed the cultural area of Mesoamerica and Arid America.

In Mexico, an ethnic group is identified by its language, the main cultural element taken into consideration in carrying out the National Population Census. For this reason, ethnic group and language can be taken as one and the same.

With this linguistic criterion as a base, 56 indigenous groups are officially recognized by the National Indigenous Institute. These groups are the direct heirs of the cultures of Mexico's glorious past, as well as of the mixture of cultures that came into being with the arrival of the Spanish conquerors.

There is a noticeable and unfortunate contrast between the great variety of archaeological pieces exhibited in the lower levels of the museum –containing elements which permit one's imagination to picture the grandeur of the urban centers and the cultural wealth achieved by the pre-Columbian peoples– and the lack of material possessions –not, however, synonymous with cultural poverty– of the large contemporary indigenous groups. The latter usually have been relegated to the least productive and most isolated parts of the country, have even been dispossessed of their lands and forced to emigrate to the cities, or have had to obtain temporary work as agricultural laborers, but they have almost always been condemned to live at a level close to the minimum needed for subsistence.

It is, in fact, perhaps remarkable that these groups have retained any aspects of their culture, despite the incredible violence to which they have been subjected during the three centuries of Spanish colonization and the more than a century and a half of consolidation of the Mexican Republic. Although it is true that a new appreciation has been shown toward the native groups within Mexico since the 1910 Revolution, it is also true that in practice little has been done to help them.

Throughout the history of Mexico, these groups have fought to defend their land through economic, social, and cultural claims.

A noticeable change has taken place in the lifestyles of these groups due to the penetration of different communications media and the opening of new roads, which has caused many natives to emigrate to the big cities. They have become bilingual because of the necessity to understand Spanish; at the same time, they have changed their traditional form of dress, adopting clothing commonly used by the masses.

According to the geography and location of the villages, houses and cultivated lands are organized in one of three types of distributions: dense, semi-dense, and dispersed. In the first, houses line the streets; in the second, houses alternate with cultivated areas; and in the third, houses are separated from one another because of the harshness of the terrain.

With few exceptions, the Indian dwelling is rectangular in shape, without windows, and consists of one room with an integrated or separate kitchen, a granary, an enclosure for animals, and a well.

Lands for cultivation are generally poor or are located on steep mountain slopes, so that crops, consisting of corn, beans, squash, and chile, are minimal. But some groups engage in the commercial production of crops such as coffee or sugarcane, among others. Ancient and rudimentary tools are still used in cultivation. To complement their economy, the people engage in the manufacture of various handicrafts, utilizing pre-Columbian and colonial techniques. The commercialization of icultural products as well as of craft takes place in the markets (tianguis) and in local markets.

Local costume or dress is a particularly distinctive trait. Many indigenous groups still use their traditional costume, and there is an incredible variety, ranging from pre-Columbian garments to modern, commercially produced clothing.

General view of the Introduction to Ethnography Hall. In the foreground is a group of Indians from various parts of the country wearing traditional dress. In the back is a granary from Tetelcingo, Morelos, called a *cuezcomate*, in which construction materials and techniques from the pre-Columbian era are still used.

MEXICO: ETHNOGRAPHIC MAP

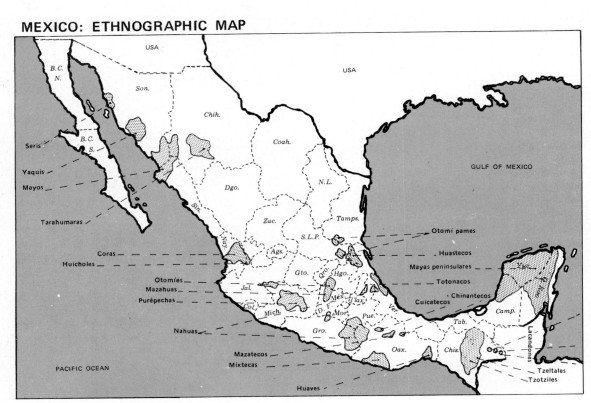

Taken from *Grupos étnicos de México*, Vol. I,
Instituto Nacional Indigenista.

Dress is so important that it serves as a means of social identification: to differentiate the wearer from the mestizo population, to announce civil status, or to give information on economic or political standing within the indigenous community.

The traditional dress used on ceremonial occasions or by those persons holding important positions in the community is very impressive.

Indigenous women like to wear a large number of necklaces and earrings to complement their dress. Today these traditional costumes have undergone great change because of the incorporation of commercial fabrics, although some still preserve their elegance and variety of colors.

Religion is very important in the Indian's life and governs social, political, and economic relations. It is usually a mixture of pre-Columbian and Catholic

Mural of graphic representation of the costumes, handicrafts, and traditions of the ethnic groups that currently inhabit different parts of Mexico. Here we find the voladores or "flyers," from Central Veracruz; the colorful costumes of the different indigenous groups living in the states of Oaxaca and Chiapas; the typical Maya *huipiles*; the Huichols with their embroidered costume and colorful hats from the mountains of Western Mexico (state of Nayarit); and the Seri navigators in the Gulf of Cortés.

beliefs. The most important religious festivities take place in honor of the village's patron saint, at Carnival and during Holy Week. All religious festivals are accompanied by music and dances that originated in pre-Columbian times and by European features acquired during the colonial period.

Society is based on the family, that is, father, mother, and children, which forms the basic unit in the social and economic organization. Often integrated into the basic nuclear family group are the sons-in-law, daughters-in-law, and grandchildren, who live in the same dwelling. The father is recognized as the supreme authority. Kin relationships sometimes extend beyond the family group to include godchildren and godparents.

Two forms of government exist: the national public administration, that is, the municipality, generally represented by bilingual mestizos; and the traditional Indian government, formed by a Council of Elders, who achieve office through outstanding performance in various civil and religious duties.

In the twelve halls occupying the upper level of the museum, aspects of the material culture of the most representative ethnic groups are shown.

The first hall offers a general view of the characteristics of Mexico's indigenous cultures. Next are examples of the dwellings, dress, handicrafts and so on, of the Coras and Huichols, groups of approximately 10,000 members each who live in the western Sierra Madre, in the states of Jalisco and Nayarit.

The following section is dedicated to the 48,000 Purépechas, who live in the mountains, on the plateau, and in the valleys of Michoacán.

At the present time, there are around 327,000 Indians speaking the Otomí language, scattered throughout isolated areas in the states of Mexico, San Luis Potosí, Hidalgo, Querétaro, Puebla, Tlaxcala, Michoacán, and Veracruz.

Between Veracruz and Puebla, in the eastern ranges of the Sierra Madre, there are four indigenous groups, which are represented in the next hall: the Nahuas, Totonacs, Otomís, and Tepehuas.

The ethnographic hall of Oaxaca is found directly above the archaeological hall for the same region. Here there are fifteen different indigenous groups, with about one million members.

Next comes the hall dedicated to the Gulf Coast (states of Tamaulipas and Veracruz), where there are various groups, outstanding among which are the Totonacs (70,000 individuals) and the Huastecs (65,000)

The Mayan groups from the highlands of Chiapas and from the lowlands of Tabasco, Chiapas, and Yucatán occupy an important section, because of the diversity of the cultures.

Some aspects of the indigenous cultures of the Northwest are shown. Here indigenous traditions and identity are preserved and are represented by display on the Tarahumaras, the Seris, the Yaquis, and the Mayos.

Finally, we find the Nahua hall, the most recently inaugurated. It is designed to show characteristic aspects of the Nahuatl-speaking population, which is probably the most widely scattered, spreading from the state of Durango to Puebla, Tlaxcala, Guerrero, Hidalgo, and the Federal District. Despite their integration into the metropolitan zone, natives of Xochimilco and the villages to the south of the Valley of Mexico and of the Ajusco mountains still preserve many aspects of the traditional culture.

Right: Huichol dress is characterized by its richly colored embroidery, consisting of stepped frets and stylized animals. Masculine dress is the more elaborate, because it is a symbol of social standing. Sierra de Nayarit.

Above: Carlos Mérida has gathered the plastic traditions of pre-Columbian and indigenous Mexico in an abstract contemporary artistic style. This mural is made of translucent plastic, with a metal framework.

Below: These polychrome stones with handsome abstract designs of symbolic significance, called *nierikas*, are offered by the Huichols to their gods.

Above: The typical Tarascan dwelling is called a *troje*. In front of the entrance is the family altar, and the porch is used as a granary, giving rise to the name which signifies "granary." State of Michoacán.

Left: Costume used in the dance of *Los Negritos,* in Uruapan, Michoacán.

139

Above: The Otomi-Mazahuas customarily build shrines in their fields, dedicated to some saint or personage of the Catholic pantheon. North-eastern Mexico State, principally.

Left: Mazahua bag embroidered with bird and flower figures.

Right: Dancers use a headdress imitating the feathers of the quetzal bird to perform the Dance of the Quetzals. Sierra de Puebla.

Above: Otomí dwelling from the Sierra de Puebla.

Below: The techniques used in the embroidery of costumes from the Sierra de Puebla are frequently of pre-Columbian origin. A *quechquémitl* from San Pablito.

Right: A Nahua woman from the Sierra of Puebla uses articles of pre-Columbian origin in her dress, such as this skirt, sash, and embroidered blouse.

Above: The Zapotecs of the Isthmus and the Valleys of Oaxaca transport their produce in wooden carts hauled by oxen.

Right: In the northern part of the state of Oaxaca, on the slopes of the eastern Sierra Madre, which descend to the Gulf of Mexico, there are around 200,000 Indians, including Mazatecs, Cuicatecs, and Chinantecs. These indigenous groups are notable for the richness, variety and color of their dress.

CHINANTECOS

CUICATECOS

MAZATECOS

Left: Headaddress used in the dance of *Las Guaguas*, typical of the region of Papantla, Veracruz.

Right: One of the most note-worthy dances of pre-Columbian origin that the Totonacs of Central Veracruz preserve is the dance of *El Volador* (The Flyer). In the upper part is a post, 30 m in height on which is placed a reel that holds the ropes sustaining the "flyers." The "flying" dancers, who are tied at the waist, leap from the top, while the principal performer dances above the reel, playing the flute and the drum.

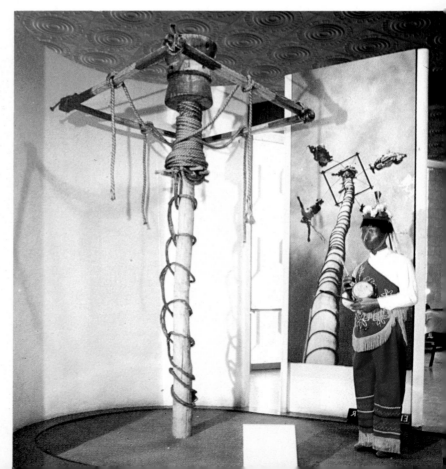

Dancing is a very important activity in the Totonac communities. This is the dress for the dance of *Los Negritos.*

Above: The Huastecs have family workshops where they make pitchers, pots, bricks, etc., in various sizes and forms. Although the ceramic ware is generally coarse, the decoration is very beautiful.

Right: The Lacandon Indians from the jungles of Chiapas belong to the Maya groups that have best preserved their language and their costumes, due to their isolation. On the wall, we see a representation of the *Balche* ceremony; below it vessels with different symbolic contents, which are used in this ceremony, placed on a kind of "cloth" of green leaves.

Above: The varied dress used by the Mayas in the highlands of Chiapas lend color to the market or *tianguis* where they take advantage of the occasion to chat with friends in addition to engaging in the commercial activity.

Above: Carnival is very important to the Tzeltals and Tzotzils of Chiapas. It retains its festive spirit and is part of the calendar of religious festivals.

The Yaquis from the state of Sonora also have traditional dances and ceremonies in which masks and costumes are used. The dance of *Pascola* gets its name from *Pascua*, or Easter, and is performed during Easter Week. To the left and right are two masks used in this dance.

Above: The tarahumaras who live in the mountains of Chihuahua perform the dance of the *Matachines* during their religious festivities. They wear capes, crowns, and mantles and carry rattles.

Upper right: The Nahua Hall was inaugurated in 1984, to celebrate the twentieth anniversary of the National Museum of Anthropology. Here we find traditional aspects of the Nahua groups who still live scattered throughout Central Mexico and in some northern states, such as Durango. These groups often coexist with the culture of great urban centers, as is the case with the Nahuas of Xochimilco and other areas near Mexico City.

Lower right: Woman weaving on a back-strap loom; Nahua family from Guerrero.

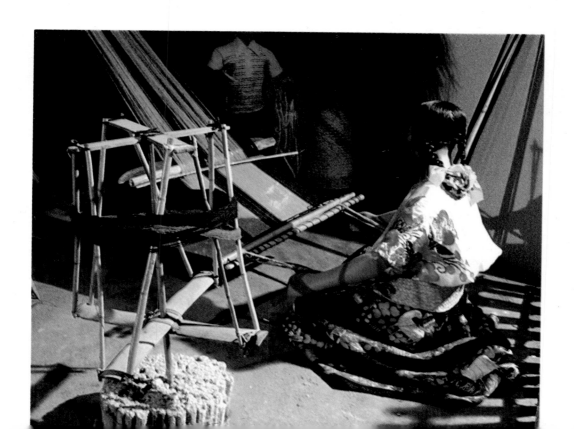

Representation of an agricultural ceremony of the Nahuas of Morelos, called "the Flower-covered" or *Periconeada.* It consists of making crosses with *pericon* flowers at the four corners of the harvest, in the orchards, in the houses, and in the *cuezcomates* or granaries, to protect these from evil.

The Nahuas of Guerrero complement their agricultural economy with various handicrafts which are made by all the members of the family. Some paint gourds or *amate* paper, others embroider, weave palm leaves, or manufacture textiles on back-strap looms.

The Nahuas of Tlaxcala also use back-strap looms to make articles of clothing, but the men make *sarapes,* coats, and tablecloths for the commercial market on wooden looms.

Above: The weekly market at Huejutla, Hidalgo, is of great economic importance. Various forms of exchange are used here, from barter to large transactions for the purchase or sale of agricultural products.

Right: The Nahuas of the Sierra de Zongolie, Veracruz, drying the coffee harvest using traditional methods.

In Tlaxcala, Carnival is very important. Communities organize fiestas where one can find different dances and groups of masked dancers, depending on the region of the state.

Bibliography

BERNAL, Ignacio, *et al.*
 1967 "Museo Nacional de Antropología", *Artes de México,* núm. 66-67, Año XII, México.

BERNAL, Ignacio, PIÑA CHAN, Román y CAMARA-BARBACHANO, Fernando
 1976 *Tesoros del Museo Nacional de Antropología de México.* Ediciones Daimon, México.

BRAMBILA, Rosa
 1984 *Teotihuacan,* Sala de Teotihuacan, Museo Nacional de Antropología. G. V. editores, México.

CARDOS DE MENDEZ, Amalia
 1983 *Los Mayas,* Sala Maya, Museo Nacional de Antropología. G. V. editores, México.

CORDRY, Donald and Dorothy
 1978 *Mexican Indian Costumes,* University of Texas Press, Austin.

GARCIA VALADES, Adrián
 1983 *Los Aztecas,* Sala Mexica, Museo Nacional de Antropología. G. V. editores, México.

INSTITUTO NACIONAL DE ANTROPOLOGIA E HISTORIA
 1967 *Museo Nacional de Antropología.* SEP/INAH, México.

 1979 *Una visión del Museo Nacional de Antropología.* SEP/INAH, México.

 1984 *Guías Salas de Etnografía, Museo Nacional de Antropología.* INAH, México.

INSTITUTO NACIONAL INDIGENISTA
 1982 *Grupos Etnicos de México.* Tomo I, INI, México.

LUDOVICO R., Carlo y RAGGHIANTI C., Licia
 1970 *National Museum of Anthropology Mexico.* Colección *Great Museums of the World,* Arnoldo Mondadori Editore, CEAM-Milán, Italy.

MATOS MOCTEZUMA, Eduardo
1979 "Las corrientes arqueológicas en México", *Nueva Antropología*, Año III, núm. 12, México.

PIÑA CHAN, Román
1960 *Mesoamérica: ensayo histórico cultural.* **Memorias VI. SEP/INAH, México.**

RAMIREZ VAZQUEZ, Pedro, *et al.*
1968 *El Museo Nacional de Antropología.* **Panorama Editorial, México.**

NOTE: In addition to consulting the bibliography cited above, a great deal of the information contained in this text comes from the Museum documentation found in the museum halls. Carolina Martínez Céspedes collaborated in the research undertaken for this book.

PHOTOGRAPHY CREDITS

GARCIA VALADES, Adrián, photographs on pages: *9, 11, 16, 17, 20 (upper), 31, 36, 41, 42, 43, 55, 57, 58, 60, 63, 64, 65, 67, 68, 74, 87, 90, 94, 96 (upper), 101, 103, 106, 107, 108, 109, 114, 115, 116, 124, 131, 133, 135, 139, 141.*

GOMEZ TAGLE, Silvia, photographs on pages: *5, 7, 19, 20 (lower), 21, 22, 23, 25, 26, 27, 28, 29, 32, 33, 34, 35, 37, 38, 39, 40, 45, 46, 47, 48, 49, 50, 51, 52, 53, 56, 59, 61, 62, 66, 69, 71, 72, 73, 75, 76, 77, 78, 79, 80, 81, 82, 83, 84, 85, 88, 89, 91, 92, 98, 99, 104, 105, 110, 111, 112, 113, 117, 120 (upper), 126, 130, 137, 138, 140, 142, 143, 144, 145, 146, 147, 148, 149, 150, 151, 152, 153, 154, 155, 156, 157, 158.*

GROBET, Lourdes, photographs on pages: *93, 95, 96 (lower). 97, 100, 119, 120 (lower), 121, 123, 125, 127, 128, 129.*